How Not to Raise a Cain

Sandy Rau and
Pat Holt, with Dave Holt

While this book is designed for the reader's personal enjoyment and profit, it is also intended for group study. A leader's guide is available from your local bookstore or from the publisher at $.75.

VICTOR BOOKS

a division of SP Publications, Inc., Wheaton, Illinois
Offices also in Fullerton, California • Whitby, Ontario, Canada • London, England

Library of Congress Catalog Card Number: 77-092291
ISBN: 0-88207-515-2

VICTOR BOOKS
A division of SP Publications, Inc.
P.O. Box 1825 • Wheaton, Ill. 60187

Contents

Preface

Dear Parents,
It's one of those days! The phone is ringing, your oldest child is quarrelsome and already complaining about having to go to Sunday School "every single Sunday," your youngest child is crying about who knows what, the television is blasting its redundant potpourri, and—it's only 10:30 A.M.

You wonder where you've gone wrong—or if you have. You've had lots of advice and opinions from your friends and read what many experts have to say, but none of it seems to help you solve your particular problems.

Or you may be just starting your family and desire to establish a God-conscious home. But you need help in setting realistic goals and standards. In either case, we believe this book can help you. The Lord has been preparing us to write this book for a long time. We have been writing together for several years, and have been asked all types of questions by readers of our weekly newspaper column, "For Parents Only." Questions of a spiritual nature pop up constantly, and we have personally observed the harmful effects of an increasing lack of spiritual interest and direction in many families. We have felt a very strong leading to provide practical information for Christian parents that will help them successfully meet their key responsibility—their children.

The purpose of *How Not to Raise a Cain* is to provide practical "how to" answers to the problems you face as parents. Each chapter formulates and provides practical methods of attaining goals that are essential in rearing children as Christians. We don't pretend to have ALL the answers, nor have we attempted to deal with all the questions you may have, but we have discussed questions that are frequently asked in our column, seminars, and personal consultation with parents. We are confident that the methods of rearing children presented here are biblically sound and have been proven successful.

We pray that this book will not only enrich the daily lives of your own family, but also the lives of others with whom you may share it.

Yours for keeping the love, joy, and peace of Christ in our families,

Sandy, Pat, and Dave

Introduction

It's your son's first "big race." He's "itching" to show how fast he can run in his tried 'n true tennis shoes.

Get ready! Get set! GO!!! And they're off! Your son is running fast, and you're cheering excitedly. Suddenly, for no apparent reason, your child hesitates, falters, stops completely, looks embarrassed, and starts crying! You wonder what could possibly be the problem.

After your child calms down, you ask him what happened. His reply is simple but profound. "I didn't know where the finish line was." Without knowing where to run, a child can't do his best in a race. And without clear objectives as parents, we cannot rear our children to reach their maximum potential.

You may be thinking, "I provide my children with food, clothing, shelter, love, understanding, and discipline. I take them to church and read Bible stories to them. Isn't that enough?" Certainly all these things are important and necessary. But biblical training involves far more, as we are instructed in Deuteronomy 6:5-7:

"Thou shalt love the Lord thy God with all thine heart, and with all thy soul, and with all thy might. And these words, which I command thee this day, shall be in thine heart; and thou shalt teach them diligently unto thy children, and shalt talk of them when thou sittest in thine house, and when thou walkest by the way, and when thou liest down, and when thou risest up."

The first principle stated in these verses is that training begins with the parents' hearts. As parents, you must first become spiritually what you want your children to be. The extent to which your own lives are not what they should be is reflected in the lives of your children. Your example sets the spiritual tone for the family and is the key to the biblical training of your children.

The second principle set forth in these verses is that you must consistently and constantly train your children. This training is not to be done spasmodically or just when it's convenient for you, but should permeate your entire family life. You can accomplish this by clearly defining your goals for the training of your family.

We believe the following goals are critical and each one is discussed in succeeding chapters.

1. Lead your children to a saving knowledge of Jesus Christ.

2. Lead your children to desire a life centered on Christ and based on God's Word.

3. Understand the importance of your task as parents and commit yourselves completely to it.

4. Teach your children how to worship God.

5. Develop the potential skills of your children in all areas, i.e. social, physical, mental, emotional, and spiritual. Develop well-rounded, stable individuals.

6. Instill in your children the habit of self-discipline.

7. Enjoy your children.

1

Just Who Is a Christian?

Is a Christian a person who goes to church every Sunday? Who looks sad and rarely smiles? Who always tries to be "good"? Who is boring, negative, and fearful? How would *you* answer these questions?

A Christian *should* be different from a non-Christian. But just because a person becomes a Christian doesn't mean that he automatically becomes perfect. It does mean he now has a "light at the end of his tunnel." For he has a new Source of energy, wisdom, motivation, and power—the Holy Spirit—dwelling inside to help him. His secret is that he now sees himself as God sees him and this fills him with joy. He has a new nature according to 2 Corinthians 5:17: "Therefore if any man be in Christ, he is a new creature; old things are passed away; behold, all things are become new."

How many times have we heard the expression, "Practice what you preach!" Many parents

prefer this one: "Do what I say, not what I do!"
Which kind of parents are we? The training we
give our children is only as effective as we are by
our examples. The first goal in raising our children should be to lead them to a saving knowledge of the Lord Jesus Christ. They need to understand that Jesus loves them, died for their
sins, and was raised from the dead.

How can we lead our children to Christ?

We hope we can, in the following pages, provide some of those answers.

Is the salvation of children the parents' responsibility?

Don't depend on your pastor or Sunday School
teacher to lead your children to the Lord. You do
it. Church and Sunday School can help, but they
should only provide a small fraction of your children's spiritual training, for this is primarily your
responsibility as parents.

Here are some ways you can help your children come to know the Lord:

1. The first prerequisite is that you must know
Jesus Christ personally as Saviour and Lord.

2. Christ must be a living reality in your own
life. The training you give to your children is
effective only as it is reinforced by your example
of Christ at work in your own life.

3. Pray for each of your children individually.

4. Know your children. Train yourself to look
for evidences in their lives that they are ready to
talk about spiritual matters. These may include:

    a. Times of stress and sorrow.

    b. Times of exceeding joy.

    c. After a time of discipline when a child is

repentant and receptive. (Please be careful not to preach or force the issue if the child is not receptive. He may think that your presentation is part of the discipline.)

5. Know how to present the plan of salvation to your children in simple terms. Some verses you should be familiar with are: John 3:16, Romans 3:23, Romans 6:23, John 1:12, Romans 5:8, John 14:6, Ephesians 2:8-9.

6. Don't assume your children are saved just because they "asked Jesus into their hearts." A young child will frequently say he wants Jesus in his heart when you ask him because it seems so nice, but he may have no comprehension of sin, its penalty, or the substitutionary death of Jesus Christ. Make sure that each of your children:

    a. Understands and believes that Jesus loves him, died for him, took his sin-punishment, and was raised from the dead.

    b. Confesses with his mouth the Lord Jesus as Saviour and Lord.

    c. Asks Jesus to forgive his sins and come into his life. In this connection explain that "sin" is a very comprehensive term, and includes everything not in the will of God for him.

    d. Understands that as a result of his trust in Jesus Christ, he will one day be with Him in heaven.

I'm not really sure my eight-year-old son is saved. How can I tell for sure?

Have you asked him? What was his reaction? Does he understand that he is a sinner who needs

God's forgiveness? (John 3:16 is one of the best verses to use with a child, substituting the child's name for "whosoever.") Does he understand God is a perfect God who cannot tolerate sin, yet loved him so much that He sent His only Son, Jesus Christ, to die on the cross for his sins? Does he understand that if he believes this, and asks Jesus to come into his heart and life, he will be forgiven for his sins, and God will then give him the Holy Spirit to live in his heart to guide and direct him? And is he certain that Jesus is preparing a place for him in heaven where he will live with Him some day?

From the time he said that he accepted the Lord Jesus Christ as his personal Saviour, did you notice a change in his life and behavior? Even though a child is young, parents often observe a behavioral and attitudinal change.

When he does something that is wrong, is he genuinely sorry for what he has done? Does he ask Jesus to forgive him and to help him do better?

Ask the Lord to give you discernment in telling if your son is saved or not. Ask Him also to give you the peace and reassurance you need if he is saved, or the wisdom to deal with him if he is not.

At how early an age can a child be saved?

The age at which a child can be saved depends on his maturity and the amount of spiritual "input" he has had. A child who, at a young age, loves Bible stories, listens attentively, and can answer simple questions is a child who may be ready to ask Jesus to "come into his heart."

Two years ago a friend spoke to a group of

three- and four-year-olds telling them very simply the "story" of John 3:16: "For God so loved the world, that He gave His only begotten Son, that whosoever believeth in Him should not perish, but have everlasting life."

She did not ask for hands, knowing that probably the hands of 99 percent of the children would go up whether or not they understood what they were doing. Just as the group began to sing a song, Kristin, a little three-and-a-half-year-old girl interrupted and said, "I want to take Jesus into my heart right now!" Interestingly enough, none of the other children in the group followed her lead. Hers was a personal and individual decision. After summer vacation, our friend spoke with the group again, and asked if any had ever asked Jesus to come into his heart. Several hands were raised. Little Kristin's hand was one of them. When she was asked to tell about her experience, she replied, "Don't you remember? It was last year when I was three that Jesus came into my heart." Jesus Christ lives in Kristin's heart though she is so young.

Of course, many young children who sincerely accept Christ as their Saviour do not fully comprehend all that is involved in salvation. But as they mature mentally and physically they will also mature spiritually, assuming they are given, and are receptive to, proper Christian training.

At what age should a child be taught about Christianity? How do I go about this?

It's never too soon to start! You can hang simple and colorful pictures of Bible stories in your baby's room near his crib or playpen. You can sing such hymns as "Jesus Loves Me" while you are feeding or changing your baby. Then as your child grows older, you can teach him the words to those hymns you've been singing to him.

As soon as your child is old enough to listen to stories, tell him Bible stories which contain easily understood lessons. Make a game of learning Bible verses together. A child of three can learn such verses as:

1 John 4:8—God is love.

1 Peter 5:7—God cares for me.

Psalm 136:1—Give thanks to God.

1 John 4:10—God sent His Son.

Hebrews 13:6—The Lord is my Helper.

Psalm 147:7—Sing unto the Lord.

When your child feels happy or especially thankful about something that's happened to him, tell him that all wonderful things are gifts from God.

A very young child can be taught to bow his head and fold his hands during prayer. As a child approaches two and a half years of age, he will want to participate in the mealtime prayer of thanks for the food, and later on, take part in bedtime prayers. Point out to the child that just by listening carefully to whoever is praying, he is really praying with the person.

Any money given to your child should be shared with the Lord. Use either a bank or a special box which you can label, "My Gift to God," or your choice of an appropriate caption. Encourage your child to place a portion of his money into the bank consistently. Be certain that this money is used for some phase of the Lord's work selected by your child under your guidance.

Most important of all is your parental example set in your home. If your home is truly committed to the Lord, your child will learn at an early age what Christianity is all about before you say a word. As you go about your daily life, pray for guidance. You'll think of many creative ways to share God's love with your youngster.

What do we say to neighbors who are reluctant to let their children go to church with us? They say that they want their children to be able to choose their own religion when they are older, and wonder if it would be a mistake to insist on their going to a special church now.

The most succinct answer to this question is found in Proverbs 22:6: "Train up a child in the way he should go; and when he is old, he will not depart from it." This includes training in attitudes toward God, church attendance, choice of religion, manners, morals, education, etc.

Are these same parents waiting until their children are old enough to decide if they really want to drink milk and eat healthful foods before feeding them? Of course not! Very young children are not capable of making a proper decision, and if permitted to decide when and what to eat, they would soon suffer from malnutrition. Neglecting the spiritual nutrition of children likewise has detrimental results.

Princess Grace has said, "Many parents do nothing about their children's religious education, telling them they can decide what they believe when they're 21. That's like telling them they can decide, when they're 21, whether or not they should brush their teeth. By then, their teeth may have fallen out. Likewise, their principles and morality may also be nonexistent." We agree!

Our son is seven years old and has attended Sunday School regularly since Cradle Roll days. We are a believing family and have had many discussions relating to "taking Jesus into your heart." However, my son still seems a bit confused about why he needs to ask Jesus into his heart. How can we explain this?

Your son needs to understand that ALL sin grieves God and that ALL children are born with sinful hearts. The best place to begin is by reading the story of Adam and Eve in the Garden of Eden where man's sin began (Gen. 3). Once your son fully understands what occurred in the Garden, elaborate on the fact that this sin nature is passed on from generation to generation and that according to Romans 6:23 the penalty of sin is death (eternal judgment).

However, because God loved us so very much He sent His Son to pay sin's penalty for us (1 Peter 2:24) and now He offers us a wonderful gift—eternal life! (John 3:16)

There is only ONE WAY we can receive this gift. Every person must accept what Christ did for him on the cross and ask Him into his heart and life.

Lead your son to a simple assurance that Jesus forgives the sins of all who accept Him into their hearts and put their trust in Him. Reviewing John 5:24 and John 1:12 will be helpful.

2

One Book
Does It All

Songs, poetry, history, love, adventure, and mystery are just a few of the ingredients in this marvelous Book. How can one Book contain so much? Simply because God wanted it to be written!

If we wanted to learn to drive a car, we would probably read a driver's manual of instruction. This manual would tell us how to start the engine of the car, how to make left and right turns, how to back the car and most importantly, the rules for driving a car. The Bible is OUR Instruction Manual. It tells us how to start our engines in tune with Christ, how to make decisions when we don't know which way to turn, how to back up and wait for God's leading and . . . what God's rules are for living our daily lives.

As Christians, the Bible is not only our Instruction Manual—it is also our food. If we love, obey, and believe in God's Word we receive sustenance for getting through this earthly life. No matter what the situation, the Bible has the answer for us.

Our responsibility as parents is to lead our children to desire a life centered in God's Word. They need to sense and observe our own deep love and commitment to the Bible and to become involved in its daily use. Our children need to be taught that the Bible is true, accurate, and infallible so that it can be trusted completely as a Guide for life. They need to learn what God has to say to them personally and to delight in it as Psalm 1:2 teaches: "But his delight is in the law of the Lord; and in His law doth he meditate day and night."

During our family devotions, whenever we attempt to discuss Jesus' coming back to earth again, our daughter becomes frightened. She is a Christian but doesn't want us to talk about Jesus' return at all. We wonder whether we've somehow made her feel that it's a day to fear rather than an event we're looking forward to. Can you give us specific suggestions for telling a child about the Second Coming?

First Thessalonians 4 and 5 reassure believers of the happy events that will occur when Jesus returns for them. "For God has not destined us for wrath, but for obtaining salvation through our Lord Jesus Christ, who died for us, that whether we are awake or asleep, we may live together with Him" (5:9-10, NASB).

Believers should not be afraid of Jesus' return because at that time He has promised to take us to heaven to live with Him.

Perhaps it would help to tell your daughter

about heaven and what a fantastically wonderful place it is! Revelation 21 and 22 give us a little glimpse of its splendors. Explain that it's been almost 2,000 years since Jesus went to heaven. He didn't tell us when He'd return—only that He would. No one knows exactly when that day will come. Reassure your daughter that because she is a believer, when that event occurs she will be with Jesus. Mention the names of family members and friends who are also believers, so she will know whom she will be with in heaven—forever! Speak enthusiastically about the day when Jesus will return, show you are joyfully looking forward to it, and your attitude will be contagious. Pray with her about any remaining fears, asking the Lord to reassure her and remove them.

Our 11-year-old daughter is very pretty but is quite vain about her appearance. She often comments to us that she is so much better looking than this or that girl. Using Scripture, how can we help our daughter deal with her pride?

God doesn't put the same value on physical attractiveness that we do. "God sees not as man sees, for man looks at the outward appearance, but the Lord looks at the heart" (1 Sam. 16:7, NASB). The Lord wants our hearts to be beautiful. "As [a man] thinketh in his heart, so is he" (Prov. 23:7).

Proverbs 27:2 reminds us to "Let another praise you, and not your own mouth; a stranger, and not your own lips" (NASB). Proverbs 16:18 warns us that "Pride goes before destruction, and a haughty spirit before stumbling" (NASB). Proverbs 6:16-17 tells us that pride is one of the things "which the Lord hates."

Your daughter needs to understand that her good looks are a gift from the Lord, as James 1:17 teaches us that "Every good thing bestowed and every perfect gift is from above, coming down from the Father of lights, with whom there is no variation, or shifting shadow" (NASB).

As soon as your daughter understands these Scriptures, help her to pray about her pride by first confessing to the Lord this sin of pride in her appearance and then by asking the Lord to remove her pride and help her to focus her attention on making her heart beautiful in God's sight.

What is involved in the term "Christian home"? My wife and I want to have one, but we see so many different types of so-called Christian homes that we aren't sure which are really based on Scripture. Can you help us?

The term, "Christian home," implies that the people in the home and all their activities are Christ-centered.

A Christian home starts with the father who is the head of the home, as taught in Ephesians 5:22-33.

Wives, submit yourselves unto your own husbands, as unto the Lord.

For the husband is the head of the wife, even as Christ is the head of the church; and He is the Saviour of the body.

Therefore as the church is subject unto Christ, so let the wives be to their own husbands in every thing.

Husbands, love your wives, even as Christ also

loved the church, and gave Himself for it;
That He might sanctify and cleanse it with the
washing of water by the Word;
That He might present it to Himself a glorious
church, not having spot, or wrinkle, or any such
thing; but that it should be holy and without
blemish.
So ought men to love their wives as their own
bodies. He that loveth his wife loveth himself.
For no man ever yet hated his own flesh; but
nourisheth and cherisheth it, even as the Lord
the church.
For we are members of His body, of His flesh,
and of His bones.
For this cause shall a man leave his father and
mother, and shall be joined unto his wife, and
they two shall be one flesh.
This is a great mystery; but I speak concerning
Christ and the church.
Nevertheless let every one of you in particular
so love his wife even as himself; and the wife
see that she reverence [respect] her husband.

The father is to be the spiritual leader of the
home. He needs to be rooted and grounded in the
Word of God, and an example of applying its
precepts in his own life, so that he can teach them
in turn to his family.

The mother is to be submissive to the father, as
he guides the home in love, wisdom, and understanding. She is the "keeper of the home," and
her life can be as varied and exciting as that one
described so beautifully in Proverbs 31:10-31:

Who can find a virtuous woman? For her price
is far above rubies.
The heart of her husband doth safely trust in

her, so that he shall have no need of spoil.

She will do him good and not evil all the days of her life.

She seeketh wool, and flax, and worketh willingly with her hands.

She is like the merchants' ships; she bringeth her food from afar.

She riseth also while it is yet night, and giveth meat to her household, and a portion to her maidens.

She considereth a field, and buyeth it; with the fruit of her hands she planteth a vineyard.

She girdeth her loins with strength, and strengtheneth her arms.

She perceiveth that her merchandise is good; her candle goeth not out by night.

She layeth her hands to the spindle, and her hands hold the distaff.

She stretcheth out her hand to the poor; yea, she reacheth forth her hands to the needy.

She is not afraid of the snow for her household; for all her household are clothed with scarlet.

She maketh herself coverings of tapestry; her clothing is silk and purple.

Her husband is known in the gates, when he sitteth among the elders of the land.

She maketh fine linen, and selleth it; and delivereth girdles unto the merchant.

Strength and honor are her clothing;   and she shall rejoice in time to come.

She openeth her mouth with wisdom; and in her tongue is the law of kindness.

She looketh well to the ways of her household, and eateth not the bread of idleness.

Her children arise up, and call her blessed; her husband also, and he praiseth her,

"Many daughters have done virtuously, but thou excellest them all."

Favor is deceitful, and beauty is vain; but a woman that feareth the Lord, she shall be praised.

Give her of the fruit of her hands; and let her own works praise her in the gates.

The woman described in Proverbs 31 is an ideal for every generation of women to follow. She cared lovingly for her husband and children, was aware of their needs, and met them with delight and understanding. She extended her loving concern to the servants (31:15), and to the poor and needy (31:20). So she also was successfully involved in numerous outside activities, which were directed by God.

The children in a Christ-centered home are to be obedient to their parents. "Children, obey your parents in the Lord; for this is right" (Eph. 6:1). They are to be reared to know and to love the Lord Jesus Christ and to serve Him with joy.

This kind of home is truly a "light" in a dark world, and attracts believers and nonbelievers alike because of its warmth, love, joy, peace, and unity. Each member is Spirit-controlled and a joy to live with!

Our 6-year-old seems to be afraid of the dark, and imagines that "scary" things are in the room and under the bed. Can you help us know how to handle his fears?

Make certain that your child does not look at books, TV programs, or movies which could cause these feelings of fear. If these kinds of things are contributing to his problem, prohibit him from seeing them, and tell him why.

After doing this, discuss with him at bedtime, and have him memorize this great fear-dispelling verse, 2 Timothy 1:7: "For God hath not given us the spirit of fear; but of power, and of love, and of a sound mind." Explain that God does not ever want His child to be afraid or frightened by anything. In your bedtime stories, use examples of brave men like David who killed a bear, a lion and, of course, Goliath. The biblical account makes it clear that David had no fear because his trust was not in himself but in the power of the living God—his own personal God. Daniel was not afraid in the lions' den because he knew that God could close the lions' mouths. This same God wants us to have that same kind of trust in Him.

After discussing and memorizing the verse, have your child pray that the Lord will help him be brave, take away his fear, and give him a restful and peaceful night's sleep.

Is there any way my wife and I can begin to prepare our boys—ages six and eight—for all the anti-God literature they will be exposed to and required to read in school?

Begin now to establish in their minds that the Bible is a true standard by which they can measure everything. Keep reaffirming that the Bible is the Word of God, and God cannot lie (Heb. 6:18). The Bible is true because it is inspired by God (2 Tim. 3:16-17). Whatever else they read may or may not be true and where it disagrees with what is taught in the Bible, it isn't true.

Point out that science books have always become "outdated" and, in many cases, appeared ridiculous a few years after they were written because of some new scientific insights or discoveries. Show that as man's learning has increased, science has had to change many of its theories which were contrary to the Bible, but that when science agreed with the Bible, no such problems were encountered. For example, the Bible teaches in Leviticus 17:11 that "the life of the flesh is in the blood," but until a few hundred years ago bloodletting (instead of our current practice of blood transfusions) was the generally accepted medical practice. In fact, George Washington was "bled" in a misguided effort to cure the illness that resulted in his death. It took men of science centuries to find out that what the Bible said about blood was accurate.

Become familiar with the creationist and evolutionist models of the origin of life. There are many excellent books available in your local Christian bookstore that give good, solid answers to evolutionary teaching. When your boys must read anti-God literature, review it with them and point out where it is wrong and why. Of course, let them realize that they must learn what is taught in school, but that such teaching must be recognized for what it is—theories, not facts— and that such theories are subject to change without notice!

Begin a family program of memorizing key Scriptures and reviewing them frequently. Apply the principles contained in those Scriptures to your own family's life-situation. According to Proverbs 9:10, this will produce wisdom in your children which will enable them to stand up to godless propaganda.

Is there a simple way to explain the difference between God, Jesus, and the Holy Spirit to my child?

One of the most effective methods is to use a simple illustration. Draw a picture of a triangle for your child. Write one name in each corner: God, Jesus, Holy Spirit. Point out that all three Persons make up the entire triangle, but that each has a separate point or part. There is only one God, but He is also Three Persons. They are like a family—Jesus is God's Son. All Three made the world and each has an important work in our daily lives. For example: God planned for our salvation by sending our Saviour into the world. When we realize our need of the Saviour, we invite Jesus to come into our hearts. When Jesus comes into our hearts, we are then indwelt by the Holy Spirit.

Our sons, ages 9 and 11, love sports. We would like them to learn some good sportsmanship verses so they can apply them in the months and years to come. Do you have any suggestions for our use?

Jim Welles, director of recreation for Cedar Mill Bible Church, Portland, Oregon has suggested 12 character-building questions—one to use per month with a verse to meditate upon and memorize each week.
ARE YOU RIGHT WITH GOD?—January
1 Peter 3:12
Rom. 6:19c
1 Cor. 1:30
Phil. 3:9

ARE YOU PRAYING?—February
   Phil. 4:6
   Eph. 6:18
   Rom. 12:12
   Rom. 12:14
ARE YOU WALKING IN THE TRUTH?—
March
   Phil. 4:8
   Eph. 4:29
   John 8:32
   Rom. 3:4
ARE YOU PATIENT AND KIND?—April
   Eph. 4:32
   1 Thes. 5:14
   2 Tim. 2:24
   Rom. 2:4
ARE YOU AVOIDING JEALOUSY?—May
   Rom. 12:3
   Eph. 4:7
   Rom. 2:11
   Gal. 5:26
ARE YOU BOASTFUL?—June
   1 Cor. 1:31
   James 4:6
   Rom. 3:27
   2 Cor. 10:17-18
ARE YOU PROUD?—July
   Eph. 4:2
   1 Cor. 4:7
   1 Peter 3:8b
   Phil. 2:3
ARE YOU SELFISH?—August
   Eph. 6:7
   1 Cor. 10:24
   Phil. 2:20-21
   Phil. 2:4

ARE YOU ANGRY?—September
  1 Cor. 13:5c
  Col. 3:13
  Rom. 12:19
  Eph. 4:26
ARE YOU JOYFUL?—October
  Phil. 4:4
  Luke 1:47
  1 Peter 1:8
  Rom. 15:13
ARE YOU LOVING?—November
  John 15:12
  1 Peter 4:8
  John 14:15
  1 Cor. 13:7
ARE YOU PEACEFUL?—December
  Phil. 4:7
  Eph. 4:3
  John 14:27
  Rom. 16:20

3

Getting Our
Act Together

A great actor or actress prepares totally for a role. He or she reads the lines from the script over and over until they are memorized, explores the personality of the character, and makes every effort to "become" the character in that particular role while the camera is on. However, once the camera is turned off, the actor or actress reverts to his or her own personality.

What about our everyday personalities? Are we different when the camera is turned off? Do we attend church every Sunday and play the part of a "good person," then return home and forget our lines until we're on camera again? The answer to these questions lies in our commitment— TOTAL commitment to the Lord. This is our primary responsibility as Christians and, most especially, as Christian parents. We have to "get our act together" in terms of priorities. Our children's cameras are running ALL the time and their training is our top priority. If we're too busy to give our children the time with us they need, we should give up some of those activities which keep us too busy to meet our children's needs.

The prerequisites for leaders in the church are given us in 1 Timothy 3:1-13. These verses show us that before a man is considered fit and responsible enough to serve in the household of God, he must first prove himself with his family. A prerequisite which stands out for overseers (elders) and deacons is "One that ruleth well his own house, having his children in subjection with all gravity. (For if a man know not how to rule his own house, how shall he take care of the church of God?) Let the deacons be the husbands of one wife, ruling their children and their own houses well" (1 Tim. 3:4-5, 12).

So if we're truly committed to the Lord, our families know it and show it. We need to earn our Academy Awards at home!

What can we say when our 11-year-old daughter tells us that "everyone else gets to do it," and that "everyone" includes Christian friends, but we feel what she wants to do is wrong?

After asking the Lord to give you a kind and gentle spirit, tell your daughter that you are not responsible for Joe, Mary, or whoever else is involved. But you love her, God gave her to you, and you are directly responsible to Him for her. Tell her that you have prayerfully considered the matter (make certain you have!), and that as a result of that consideration, you believe that this is not right for her to do. Explain the reasons for your decision as best you can. Admit to her that you know you are not perfect parents; you make mistakes as all parents do. But before God, you do your very best as He enables you, and in this case, you must say, "No!"

I feel as though I am saying, "No!" and "Don't do . . ." all the time. I don't know what to do about my negative responses.

The "negative trap" is a common problem which keeps many parents from enjoying their children. But by using some self-discipline and changing your approach, you can experience dramatic results in your home.

NEVER say "no!" unless you have to, but when you do say it—mean it! Have as few rules as possible, but enforce them. Many families have only simple safety rules—all else is "played by ear" until a problem arises. At that time a rule is established. The children see the need for the rule, and are more likely to abide by it without resenting it.

Your approach should be positive rather than negative. For example, instead of saying, "Don't eat any cookies before dinner," it is better to say, "You may have cookies after dinner. You'll need to wait until then."

Instead of saying, "Don't touch anything on that shelf," try saying, "If you need anything on that shelf, I will help you. You may touch the things over there."

Instead of saying, "Don't play with that now," try saying, "You may play with this right now, but you will have to wait until tomorrow (or whenever) to use that."

Instead of saying, "Don't ever do that again," it is more effective to say, "In this house we never do that. From now on you will need to remember that."

You are really saying the same thing, but in a far more palatable manner. It takes thought and time to develop the skill of being positive rather than negative in your relationship with your children, and others as well, but it is worth it.

The key to the success of this approach is that you say things *very* nicely but firmly. If you mean what you say, and the children know that if your admonition is violated there won't be a lot of talking, shouting, screaming, or multiple warnings, but you will take immediate action, many of your problems will be eliminated. When your children really know this, it is amazing how kind and gentle you can be and yet get the results you want with just a word or a look.

So—be positive, but be firm! These make a super twosome! And as a bonus your children will learn that the Christian life is basically positive rather than negative! Hooray!

My five-year-old son is sick at least once a week with a bad cold or asthma attack. He's such a sweet child that I have difficulty understanding why the Lord would allow him to suffer this way. Why does the Lord allow an innocent child to suffer? How can I help my son accept his illness in a Christian manner? Can you give suggestions to help me better endure this situation?

We often find it difficult to understand why there is pain and suffering in the world, even though we know God uses ALL circumstances for our edification. One of the most helpful verses we've found when dealing with our own physical suffering is Romans 8:28: "And we know that all things work together for good to them that love God, to them who are the called according to *His purpose.*"

It's so easy to thank God when things are going well, but when we're suffering physical and/or mental anguish, we find it very difficult to be thankful. But we believe difficulties are God's way of testing and strengthening our faith: "My brethren, count it all joy when ye fall into divers temptations [various testings]; knowing this, that the trying of your faith worketh patience. But let patience have her perfect work, that ye may be mature and perfect [complete], lacking nothing" (James 1:2-4).

Some of us have to lie flat on our backs for a long time before we realize that where we should be is on our knees. For those who are believers, we are taught to yield ourselves more fully to the Lord when we suffer. If we grumble and complain when we're suffering, we aren't yielding to His will, but we are providing a stumbling block for nonbelievers.

The Lord often uses illness or suffering as a means of bringing nonbelievers to Himself. Our cheerful and prayerful acceptance of difficult circumstances can help nonbelievers realize what being a Christian is all about.

In your particular situation we suggest that you claim 1 Thessalonians 5:16-18 in your daily prayers: "Rejoice always; pray without ceasing; in everything give thanks; for this is God's will for you in Christ Jesus" (NASB).

A sick child is truly a difficult burden to bear mentally and physically. Knowing it is God's will for you to give up many things you'd like to do in order to nurse him may not make it any easier. When you feel discouraged and frustrated, confess these feelings to the Lord and ask Him to help you be thankful for what this situation is bringing about in your character and in your life.

Your son is quite young and no doubt has difficulty understanding why the Lord is "picking on him," as one of our children claimed during a long, serious illness. All children sometimes feel that they're being punished and can't understand why God would do this to them when they've tried so hard to "be good." A child needs to understand that "the Lord is gracious and compassionate" (Ps. 111:4, NASB), and He has promised that in heaven "He shall wipe away every tear from their eyes; and there shall no longer be any death; there shall no longer be any mourning, or crying, or pain; the first things have passed away" (Rev. 21:4, NASB).

Tell your son about Jesus' suffering and how God showed His love for us through what He did with His Son. Jesus was truly perfect, "good," and without any sin. Yet He suffered more than any of us will ever suffer because of His heavenly Father's plan for us. Perhaps God has a special plan for your son's future in which he will need to have a great deal of empathy, insight, and understanding for the problems of others and God may be helping him learn lessons through his illness that will prepare him for this. If your son can pray about his future calling, he may be able to accept his present suffering.

What is the best way to handle a situation when a ten-year-old child starts saying he doesn't want to come to church?

The "going to church" problem is one that 99 percent of all Christian parents face at some time. It is not an easy problem to deal with, partly because we as Christian parents are often so emotionally involved that we fail to make a thoughtful response, but begin the "nag" routine instead.

The five reasons most commonly used for not wanting to go to church are:

1. "I'm too tired on Sunday morning."

Satan seems to see to it that even if we are accustomed to waking up at 6:00 A.M. every other day of the week, getting out of bed by 7:00 A.M. on Sunday is a real struggle. As a family, pray on Saturday night that the Lord will give you all a restful night's sleep, and will help you to get up and get ready on Sunday morning.

Check to make certain that your children are getting to bed at a reasonable hour on Saturday night—that's YOUR responsibility and it's imperative. If you or your children have Saturday night activities, plan to leave early enough to allow time for adequate rest. If you have a babysitter, select one who is able to follow through with your suggested bedtime.

2. "I don't like my teacher. He (she) is so boring!"

Parents, let's be honest. Your child is probably correct! Not every teacher along life's road is going to be great, or even good. Many will be sincere and dedicated people who are mediocre communicators. But—the amazing thing is that God has promised in Isaiah 55:11 that He will bless the teaching of His Word, and He does! Point this out to your child; then start praying that his teacher will become more interesting and learn to present things in a more practical and inspiring way. Remind your child that he will only have this teacher for a little while, and if the students in the class would be a little more verbal in answering questions and participating, the class would be a lot more interesting. If your child tells you his teacher only lectures and gives no opportunity for discussion, you may wish to talk about this with the teacher, and suggest a more participatory approach.

Many of us can look back to our childhood and recall only a handful of good teachers. Many great teachers recalled painful sessions with boring teachers of their own, and determined to be the antithesis of such teachers. Explore with your child just what he would do if he were the teacher.

3. "I want to go somewhere else just for this Sunday—OK—Please???"

The answer is a firm, loving, "No!" Once you give in, you've broken the habit, and it's really tough to establish it again. Just tell your child that going "wherever" sounds like a great idea (if it in fact does), and maybe he can go after church, or perhaps next Saturday! Then make certain he does get to go!

Remind your child that the Lord wants us to meet with other Christians and worship together. Share Hebrews 10:25: "Not forsaking the assembling of ourselves together." So it really isn't a decision that we even have to make—the Lord has made it for us. We are to go to church to worship God, we go on Sunday, and we go as a family.

4. "None of my friends go to church."

First, you can probably mention some of his friends who do go to church, some of whom may even be in your church and/or in his class! As for the rest of his friends who do not go to church, they are probably not saved and desperately need to know our Lord and Saviour Jesus Christ personally. Your child should lose no time in praying for his friends by name and in asking the Lord to use him to bring them to know the Lord. Pray with him that he will be brave, strong, full of courage, and able to invite a friend or two to church as the Lord leads.

To make it easier for him to get his friends to go to church with him, consider making a day of it by inviting the unsaved friends not only to come to church but also to eat and play at your home all afternoon. People who do this find that the attendance is *FAR* more regular than the "pick him up, drop him off" pattern. Sure it takes a lot of extra time, but it is an investment in eternity!

5. "I don't have any friends at church."

If not, why not? Parents, point out the principle stated in Proverbs 18:24 to your child: in order to have friends, we must be friendly. Then pray together that the Lord will help him be friendly and that God will give him a special friend. If your child evidences the slightest interest in anyone in his class, get the child's name, address, and telephone number, and contact the parents to see if you can get the two together for an afternoon. Perhaps taking the child to your home after Sunday services would be convenient. This area is crucial. We all need and want friends, and must have them at church if attendance is to be enthusiastic. Commit this daily to the Lord, and be alert for His answer.

We have two children of our own, and have been considering taking a foster child or two into our home. What is your opinion?

This is an extremely serious decision and there are several things to prayerfully consider:

1. The Lord has given you two children for whom you are responsible to love, care for, nurture, and train. You must not neglect your children in order to care for foster children. Caring for foster children will detract from the time you have for your own children. Your own children might be resentful of this, particularly if the foster children are about the same age as your own. This resentment and jealousy often leads to excessive bickering. Generally speaking, it is better if the foster children are at least three years older or younger than your own children.

2. You must carefully prepare your family for foster children, because most foster children bear deep emotional scars. Your children will need to know that the foster children will require extra time and attention from you. Also, they may have come from homes where Jesus did not have priority, and where the language and actions were not honoring to Him. In addition, your children should be prepared for the possibility of withdrawal or hyperactivity by the foster children.

3. With the double responsibility of devoting sufficient time to both your own children and the foster children, you must be prepared to sacrifice some of your own outside activities in order to give all of the children the time they should have.

4. If—after prayerful consideration and discussion with your family—you still desire to have foster children in your home, then do it! You will be participating in a very needed ministry and, God willing, a fruitful one.

Is it enough to take our children to church on Sundays and send them to a Christian school?

Definitely not! What goes on in your home is what will make all the difference in their hearts and lives. Church is important. The Bible has told us not to forsake "the assembling of ourselves together" (Heb. 10:25). Christian schools do provide a base of biblical training and an outstanding opportunity to have friendships with believers. But according to Deuteronomy 6:6-7, the *major* portion of training is to be done in the home.

Home is where your children's attitudes and values are formed. Home is where your children spend the majority of their time. Home is their security, stability, and base of all operations. If you do not have family and/or individual devotions at home, and if the Lord is not talked about as if He were indeed a Member of your family, Christianity cannot become real and personal to your children on a daily basis. It will merely be something they "put on" like a Sunday jacket or pair of shoes, or something they will be able to "turn on" when they are around a certain group of people and "turn off" when around a different set of people. It will be a shallow kind of Christianity that the world will sneer at and it will not draw others to Christ and the abundant life He offers.

The kind of Christian who makes an impact on the world for Jesus Christ is one who is God-conscious and God-reliant every moment of each day.

Our one-and-a-half-year old is like a little sponge, taking in ideas and learning things. It's exciting, but a little scary too. We read somewhere that a child's values are learned by a very early age. Is this true?

Research tells us that 50% of a child's attitudes and habits are established by the time he is four years old, and that 80% of his values and attitudes are established by the time he is eight. Do not ever underestimate the importance of what you are able to teach a child every day of his first months of life—long before he is able to say, "Mommy, Daddy, I love you!"

The following poem captures the impressionableness of a child's early years.

I took a piece of plastic clay
And idly fashioned it one day
And as my fingers pressed it still
It moved and yielded at my will.

I came again when days were past,
The bit of clay was hard at last.
The form I gave it, it still bore
And I could change that form no more.

I took a piece of living clay
And gently formed it day by day
And molded with God's power and art
A young child's soft and yielding heart.

I came again when years were gone
A man now I looked upon
And he that early impress wore
And I could change him never more.
                                        —Anonymous

Should "mottos," verses, sayings, and so forth be hung around the home as part of Christian training?

It's not what's hanging on the wall, but what is in your heart and life that will permeate your home and influence your children. Plaques with verses and mottos are fine and can be helpful as long as they express the true character of your home.

My wife is not a believer and does not attend church with me and my son. My son is now six years old and cannot understand why his mommy doesn't go with us. What can I tell him? My wife doesn't object to our going but says she doesn't feel she needs such beliefs for her daily life.

This is a difficult question to answer so we asked several in similar situations for their suggestions:

Explain to your son that "we know what God wants us to do because we've learned about it at church and through reading our Bible. Mommy hasn't learned yet what God wants her to do so we'll have to pray for her to do so."

Another explanation might be: "Mommy hasn't learned to love the Lord the way we have, so we have to set a good example for her. When we are loving and kind, we are showing her how loving our Lord is. If we occasionally tell her what we believe, perhaps she'll begin to understand how much she is missing."

Your example is the best example she has of what the Lord can do in her life. Ephesians 5:25-31 gives husbands instructions as to how their wives should be treated. Treasure these verses for the guidance they can give you.

We have two children, ages four and six. They are adopted. We have not told them. Should we?

The Bible tells us in Romans 12:17b to "Provide things honest in the sight of all men." We believe that children should be told early that they are adopted and be made to feel proud of this honor. You certainly would never want them to hear from a friend who accidentally slipped it out—especially in their teen years. This could be catastrophic!

You could tell them that you wanted children very much but that God did not give you your very own children, but gave you the desire to have other children. He then provided, in His own time, "You two wonderful children. We loved you from the very start, when you were just a few days old." Share stories with the children about how they were as babies, etc. As far as the natural parents are concerned, tell only what you feel needs to be said.

Ask the Lord to reveal to you His timing for sharing this news. Very often the children will bring it up themselves, by telling about a friend at school or in the neighborhood who is adopted.

Last year my three-year-old wanted to know what she could give Jesus for His birthday at

Christmastime. I really didn't know what to tell her. Do you have any ideas?

How wonderful that a three-year-old would feel so close to the Lord! Just explain that Jesus is now in heaven so we can't wrap up a present and give it to Him. But our Bible teaches us that Jesus wants another kind of present from us . . . things we can DO! For example, He wants us to read about Him in the Bible, talk to Him often in prayer, be kind to others, love Him in our hearts, have only good words coming out of our mouths, do any job we have well, and tell others about Him.

Finding a good baby-sitter seems to be difficult for us. Any ideas?

Selecting the right "sitter" is an important family matter. Here are some guidelines that we think will help you choose more wisely.*

Start looking for a baby-sitter in your own church. Many churches and Christian schools maintain a list of competent young people and "grandmotherly-types" who want this kind of work. When you are interviewing your potential baby-sitter consider:

1. Appearance. Is she clean? Overweight to the extent it will make it difficult to care for the children?

2. Physical problems. Is she hard of hearing? A slight hearing problem is not serious, but a sitter must be able to hear your children's comments and requests . . . and a small child's cry. Are there

---

*Published in the November, 1976 issue of *Family Life Today*.

any serious health problems: heart trouble, diabetes, tendency to faint, etc.?

3. Silent or talkative? A person who is too silent may not be able to communicate friendliness or to provide a child with sufficient stimulation. On the other hand, a person who talks too much may be overpowering for a child. There is a happy medium that you will easily recognize after an interview or two.

4. Attitude about housework. It's better for a sitter to give the children full attention than ignoring them so she can give the kitchen floor one more mopping. If you do want her to do light chores make certain to define exactly what you want done.

5. Gripes and complaints. Does she discuss former employers, making negative remarks? This may be a clue that she is hard to get along with. DO listen carefully to her comments, however, since they are good clues to her attitudes, likes and dislikes.

6. Pets. If you have a pet, make sure the potential baby-sitter doesn't object and/or isn't allergic to it.

7. Salary. Be specific in your discussion about what you expect to pay. Listen to what the sitter expects to receive. If you feel her demands are unreasonable, tell her, but DO be willing to pay what is fair.

8. Pray. Before you talk with a potential baby-sitter and after your interview, pray about your decision. Ask the Lord to help you in your choice. Remember His Word says, "Ask, and it shall be given you; seek, and you shall find; knock, and it shall be opened unto you" (Matt. 7:7).

9. Help your children. When you have chosen

a sitter, take time to help your youngsters under-stand what is happening in your family. Explain when the sitter will be coming. Tell the children when you will be coming home. Provide time for the children to begin to get acquainted with the sitter before you leave.

You will be surprised at how well children re-spond to a new person in the home when you, your children, and the baby-sitter are adequately prepared.

4

Is Once a Week Enough?

If we wanted to learn a foreign language, we would probably attend a class once or twice a week and dutifully purchase whatever books were needed in preparation. Then what? Would we take the books home and leave them on a shelf to grow dusty? Would we attend our weekly class and then go home and forget about it? Or . . . would we study several times a week, practicing and reinforcing what we had learned? Practicing on a daily basis would help us learn the language even faster. To learn to do something well requires reinforcement.

Our children attend school five days a week, but only have the opportunity to attend Sunday School one day a week. What happens in between? We can't rely on the church alone to teach our children how to love and worship God. We need to reinforce spiritual concepts at home. Children can forget from week to week what they've learned in Sunday School unless worship is a daily practice. Talking to God at mealtimes and bedtimes will be equally as foreign as a foreign language without daily practice.

Daily reinforcement is necessary in order to teach our children to be God-conscious on a daily basis. Family worshiptime should be filled with praise, thanksgiving, and rejoicing as Psalm 107: 21-22 directs: "Oh that men would praise the Lord for His goodness, and for His wonderful works to the children of men! And let them sacrifice the sacrifices of thanksgiving, and declare His works with rejoicing."

At what age can you start teaching a child about God?

When a child is old enough to understand words and directions is the ideal time to begin teaching him about God!

In the morning—if the weather is lovely—you can say as you lift your wee one out of the crib and raise the shade or pull the curtains, "Just look at the beautiful day God gave us." If it is rainy you might say, "God sent us rain today for the plants and trees and flowers, for the fish in the streams and lakes, and so that we can have water to drink. Isn't it wonderful how God gives us water?" You might sing the old favorite song with your child which he may have already learned at church. "Oh who can make a _____(tree, cloud, raindrop, flower, etc.), I'm sure I can't, can you? (pointing to the child) Oh who can make a _____ (whatever), No one but God 'tis true" (pointing upward).

At prayertime, encourage him to thank God for at least one thing that is very special to him that

God has provided—Mommy, Daddy, Grandma, Grandpa, a kitten, dog, bird, friend, neighbor, trip somewhere, etc. This helps to make your child God-conscious, and he will begin to realize that whatever he has, and whatever happens to him is from the Lord.

Little ones love to learn and talk about themselves. You might say to your child, "What pretty eyes you have! What color are they? Who gave you your big beautiful blue (brown, green, etc.) eyes?" With a little encouragement, the child will answer, "God did." This kind of approach can be used with such things as his hair, teeth, nose, ears, mouth, legs, or arms. It is a little fun game that your tiny tot will enjoy playing again and again.

Start teaching about the love of God. You might ask, "Who loves you?" The child will respond with Mommy, Daddy, brother, sister, Grandma, etc. Then ask, "But who loves you even more than they?" Soon the child will learn that it is God who loves him better than anyone else ever can.

While walking in your garden at home, or along a street, look for the things God has made. All of nature testifies to the fact of God, and you will want to point this out. *Please* don't sermonize, or make a big deal out of it. Just short little examples, such as those we have mentioned, and then—on to something else. The idea is that all through your day, in whatever you do, there is a God-consciousness and awareness of Him and of what He has created, and of His love and His care. Just short little comments are sufficient for a tiny child. The little one will get the message loud and clear!

How do you have devotions with little ones, ages three and almost two?

You can have short, cuddly, story times ending with a round of sentence prayers. Kenneth N. Taylor's *The Bible in Pictures for Little Eyes* is very helpful. There is a picture for each short story that will take only a couple of minutes to read. Simple questions to ask your children are included with each story. Even if your younger child doesn't always grasp everything, he will want to be included in the comfortable security of being with you rather than in his crib alone.

Our daughter is a new believer but becomes quite upset when she has done something wrong. She doesn't know how to pray for forgiveness and feels Jesus won't love her anymore. We don't really know how to help her pray about this. Can you help?

If your daughter is a new believer she should understand that her sins have already been forgiven—that Jesus loves her no matter what she has done or will do and He now lives within her. However, she does need to confess any sin she commits in her new life, as the Bible directs in 1 John 1:9: "If we confess our sins, He is faithful and just to forgive us our sins, and to cleanse us from all unrighteousness."

One method you might use in praying with your daughter is to pray first, telling Jesus how much you and your daughter love Him, and thanking Him for what He has done for you both. Thank Him also for forgiving your sins when you

confess them to Him, and when you are genuinely sorry for what you have done. Then let
your daughter pray, telling what she did and asking the Lord to help her not to do it again. If she
is hesitant to pray aloud alone, ask her to repeat
after you and then lead her in prayer.

Once she has committed this concern to the
Lord, ask her, "Did God promise to forgive your
sins when you confess them? Did you confess
your sin? Then God has forgiven you, hasn't
He?" Remind her that in Psalm 103:12 God has
promised to remove our sins "as far as the east is
from the west."

*My two-year-old is very willing to say her
prayers some nights and other nights says, "No!"
Do I insist? I usually just ask her if she wants to
pray and if she isn't willing then I just say, "OK."*

Good for you. Your two-year-old is asserting her
independence, not rejecting the Lord. She may
be just too tired to pray. You might say, "God
loves to listen to our prayers so I will talk to Him
and you can listen tonight." Or you might ask her
if she would like to pray what you pray and repeat after you.

*My husband and I don't really have much in the
way of family devotions, and don't know how to
start or what to start with. Our children are two,
five, and seven.*

Children of all ages love stories. Why not begin
by calling your special familytime together
STORYTIME? Decide on the best time of the
day for your family. Many people prefer the early
morning after breakfast when the family is to-

gether before the day "officially" begins. Others prefer the quiet time at night before the youngest children go to bed. The Lord will help you decide which is the best time for you. Once you establish a time, stick to it. During this time phone calls will have to go unanswered if you really want your children to realize the significance you place on this time together.

There are a variety of ways to approach STORYTIME. Let's consider three of them as a start.

1. Read a story from the Bible or from an illustrated Bible storybook. After reading the story ask each child one question from the story commensurate with the child's age and ability. This helps to establish the significance of the story in each child's mind. Then kneel together as a family, and let each person pray aloud. If possible, let the father read the story, ask the questions, and close in prayer.

2. The oldest child can read a passage from the Bible—a story, a favorite psalm, or whatever he chooses. Then the father (or the oldest child) can ask each member of the family a question regarding the portion of Scripture. This is again followed by a round of family prayer.

3. A Bible story is read aloud by the father. Then, each member of the family asks one other member of the family a question about the passage. The time is closed by having each one of the family lead in prayer.

You may wish to vary the format for various days of the week, but do have a regular program. The above approaches to family devotions are short, simple and can be expanded as your family matures.

How can I handle mealtime prayer situations?
My husband is not a Christian.

Although your husband is not saved, he is the head of your home, and you want to follow this biblical principle. If possible, privately ask him if it would be OK with him if the children thank God aloud for the food before the family eats. Generally, this is acceptable to an unsaved father. Then at each meal one or more of the children can offer a simple prayer of thanks, and your husband will not be embarrassed nor will he lose his position of authority in the home.

If he is reluctant to ask the children to pray, then with his permission, simply establish a custom whereby one of the children returns thanks aloud before each meal without being asked.

What do I as a believer do to encourage daily
devotions with my child since my husband is a
nonbeliever? My husband doesn't object to our
going to church, but he doesn't wish to partici-
pate in any devotions.

First Peter 3:1-2 tells wives to "Be submissive to your own husbands so that even if any of them are disobedient to the Word, they may be won without a word by the behavior of their wives, as they observe your chaste and respectful behavior" (NASB). Since your husband prefers not to participate in family devotions, no effort should be made to "shame" him into doing so. However, you can still read the Bible and pray with your youngster without including your husband. If this means that you have to get up earlier in the morning, set your alarm clock and do it. Your child needs your spiritual leadership since he isn't receiving this guidance from his father.

If your husband objects to your having any devotions, meditate upon the above verses often for strength, and then do as he wishes. This doesn't mean that you can't use your private time with your child to talk about God's love for him. Nor does this mean that you can't share Scripture verses you've memorized with your child. You can also read your child a Bible story at bedtime and/or encourage him to read the Bible for himself. Many mothers we know are able to share their love for the Lord daily with their children without going against their husbands' wishes. Commit this situation to the Lord and He will show you the best way to proceed.

What do I say when my child says that God doesn't answer his prayers?

Share with your child the following possible reasons why his prayers may not seem to be answered:

1. Read together Psalm 66:18: "If I regard iniquity in my heart, the Lord will not hear me." Explore the possibility with your child that he may have some unconfessed sin that he needs to confess to the Lord and ask His forgiveness.

2. Read together James 4:3: "Ye ask, and receive not, because ye ask amiss, that ye may consume it upon your lusts." Perhaps your child is in the habit of asking for things that he wants for himself for selfish reasons. Analyze together his requests that have not been answered and discuss any that fall into this category.

3. Read together 1 John 5:14-15 and John

16:24: "And this is the confidence that we have in Him, that, if we ask anything according to His will, He heareth us; and if we know that He hear us, whatsoever we ask, we know that we have the petitions that we desired of Him" (1 John 5:14-15).

"Hitherto have ye asked nothing in My name; ask, and ye shall receive, that your joy may be full" (John 16:24).

Explain to your child that praying "in Jesus' name" does not mean merely tacking that phrase on to the end of our prayers, but requires a conscious effort to determine what Jesus really wants. In many cases, of course, we don't know exactly what God's will is and sometimes God answers "No!" to what we are asking in our prayers because it is not "according to His will."

We sometimes ask God to do things which are not best for us. Explain to your child also that God answers prayers in His own time—the best time, and therefore, we may have to wait for a specific answer to our prayer. It may be helpful to have your child write down prayer requests and record when and how God answered those requests.

Above all, encourage your child to continue praying because we have this promise: "The effectual, fervent prayer of a righteous man availeth much" (James 5:16).

5

Balance
Is Beautiful

Which weighs more, a ton of feathers or a ton of bricks? The answer to this tricky little question lies in recognizing the importance of balance. One ton is one ton, no matter what! We also need to recognize the importance of balance in raising our children. In order to produce well-balanced individuals, equal emphasis should be placed on the spiritual, physical, social, mental, and emotional aspects of our children's personalities.

For example, a diamond is almost universally admired for its beauty and value. A skilled craftsman must first cut and polish it with the proper tools in order to produce a sparkling gem. The more facets a diamond has, the more it sparkles and the higher its value.

The Lord has given us "diamonds in the rough"—our children. We are the craftsmen whose goal is to cut as many balanced facets into our children's personalities as possible. The more facets we develop, the more our children will "shine" and be of value. It is our responsibility to maximize the potential in each of our children. As one diamond manufacturer frequently reminds us, "A diamond is forever."

How can we deal with the TERRIBLE influence of the neighborhood children?

This is an extremely difficult but prevalent problem, and, as the American family further disintegrates, will undoubtedly become more difficult. On the lighter side, we asked our seven-year-old, "If you were a Christian father, how would you handle such a situation?" Gary promptly replied, "I would move, and if I couldn't do that, I would pray that the neighbors would!" Now in certain cases, this might be the way to resolve the problem, but let's consider a few other possibilities.

You need to prepare your children for what they are facing: namely, that these neighborhood children do not know or love our Lord, and that is why they use the bad language and do the very naughty things they do. Romans 1:21-32 tells us that this is what we can expect from those who do not know Him. Your family, on the other hand, is going in a totally different direction—in this life and the next. The Lord does not want us to do or say the naughty things that others are doing and saying, because these things are displeasing to Him.

If your children do or say wrong things, you will want to discipline and correct them because you love them so very much and care for their future. As a part of your family preparation for coping with the problem, spend time daily in the

Word and in prayer. Remember by name these neighborhood children and their parents in prayer, and pray that individually, and as a family you will be a witness to them each day in all you do and say.

Help your children realize that God has placed you in this neighborhood, and He has also placed these children and their families here. It may be His will for you to reach them for the Lord Jesus Christ. If so, this outreach probably won't be short and easy, but He will be with you each step of the way.

Perhaps you fear for the safety of your home and your children. Here is a verse to discuss and memorize as a family: "He shall give His angels charge over thee, to keep thee in all thy ways. They shall bear thee up in their hands, lest thou dash thy foot against a stone" (Ps. 91:11-12). The Lord will keep you and protect each of you in your particular situation. Billy Graham's book *Angels* recalls some fantastic examples of the Lord keeping various families in safety under seemingly impossible situations.

Your neighborhood children may have many hours of unsupervised activities when they are left home alone to their own devices. Do *NOT* allow your children to play inside their homes when no adult is present. You may not wish to allow your children to play inside their homes even when an adult is present. This is up to you. You know the entire situation. Let the Lord guide you in that decision. Invite one or two neighborhood children at a time to your home to play with your children. Try to keep your family in the majority—it's far easier to control with the numbers on your side in your own home.

At first you may find it helpful to promise neighborhood children treats (chocolate chip cookies, a popsicle, or whatever the children think is terrific) if they behave themselves satisfactorily for a given number of minutes. If the children are old enough, perhaps they could help you make the treat.

But please set your standards for behavior before the children cross your threshold. Be positive. Be friendly. Be firm. Then use the snacktime as a way of listening to the children and asking them questions. At this time begin to share with them about your family—why you do things the way you do. Eating and discussing always go well together—at any age! The children will also appreciate your time and attention, but don't expect them necessarily to express it. Keep these sessions short and sweet. If you sense a problem developing, handle it immediately. At first you may even have to ask a child to leave. But—pretty soon the word will filter through the neighborhood that you're "awfully strict, but kinda nice, and you give good treats."

After the neighborhood children leave, discuss with your own children what went on. Mention the positive things that happened—why you did and said what you did, and why you appreciate what your children said or did. Together thank the Lord for helping you through this situation, and ask for His continued wisdom and guidance in handling the next one.

Then when your family goes bike-riding or to a church picnic, or whatever, invite a child or two from the neighborhood to go along. Their parents will usually be delighted, and so will the children. Make certain you establish your standards for their behavior before you leave your driveway, and stick to them.

By doing these things, you are establishing that your home is a very desirable place to be, where lots of neat things happen. But of course, ONLY people who can behave themselves are invited! When they come to your home, they've got to be good, or else—they can't get the goodies—and the goodies include food, fun, and a sympathetic listening ear!

After building a relationship of friendship and trust with the children, invite them to come to church with you. Before they come make sure that your children have prepared the teacher and class to be especially friendly, and really make them feel welcome.

This approach has worked in many cases that we know of, and can work for you. You may very well be the Lord's instrument to change the hearts and lives of the children in your neighborhood. God has the power to change lives regardless of the situation. He has done it in the past. He had His own children living in Ephesus, Corinth, and Rome. He can do it today in your town. Trust Him to do it.

My 10-year-old son has taken up tennis, and wants to play in local junior tournaments. I think he will do very poorly. Would it be a good idea for him to face such possible crushing defeat? He is a Christian.

Before her death in 1967, Maureen Connally Brinker, the great former women's champion, who was deeply involved in junior programs said, "Any child should start playing when he has the physical strength, the concentration ability, and the sincere desire to play other than in his weekly lessons. Tournaments? By all means, as long as it remains fun, and winning does not become the all-consuming thought."

It's just as important for children to learn how to lose as how to win graciously, and to understand that progress in any sport or game is made only through a series of both wins and losses. A child who played his best must realize that others were better. Emphasize that there can be only one winner, and if there were no losers there could be no tournament. Instill in your child the realization that to lose is no disgrace, and that the real disgrace is the unwillingness to compete. As long as the determination to improve remains uppermost, there are seldom long-lasting ill effects from a defeat—unless the parents have placed an overemphasis on winning and not enough stress on the importance of learning the game and developing as a person and as a competent player.

Preparing your child through both practice and prayer before a match is important. Caution him against praying "that I'll win." Perhaps the Lord has something better to teach him at this time through losing. He may need more practice, and then, too, his gracious attitude about losing and about giving fair calls could be such a testimony to the other players that it would give him an opportunity to witness. Perhaps the Lord is teaching him patience—that life does not consist of one big win after another in any area, and that part of maturity is this realization. Perhaps the other player was so much better that your child did not deserve to win. Pray with your child that he will be able to concentrate, and that the Lord will enable him to play his very best, and that he will be a testimony to all who see him play.

How do you deal with a child who is in the "No!" stage?

It sounds like you may very well have a two-year-old! A very wise Christian woman and mother of eight, Allegra Harrah, once said, "Your child has the right to be two years old for 365 days just as you have the right to be the age you are for one entire year."

The Lord is going to teach both you and your little one much during this year. Your attitude will make the difference whether this year is a pain or a pleasure.

Right now your child is in the stage of finding out who's really in charge. Make certain he does! As far as saying, "No!" is concerned, your little one is asserting his independence from his limited vocabulary. This is really quite necessary. After all, you don't want to raise a "wet noodle." Ask yourself why your child is saying no. If it is just for defiance, clearly state the consequences of disobedience, and then, if and when your child disobeys, administer discipline as you promised. In so doing, you will find that this stage will be much abbreviated!

What are your thoughts on my children's friendships—with the saved and the unsaved?

There are three basic kinds of friendships: The first is rather superficial and is really more of a greeting acquaintance. The second is that of companionship, and the third is the deep, personal relationship that David and Jonathan shared. This last kind is the type of friendship that sustains, comforts, and encourages even during a person's hardest times.

As Christians, both our children and we as parents can enjoy friendships of the first two kinds with Christians and non-Christians alike, but the deep, abiding friendships of the third type are really only possible with other Christians who believe as we do.

We want to cultivate friendships with non-Christians because we covet them for the Lord Jesus Christ, and want to demonstrate His love and concern for them. We need to make this clear to our children.

But the most important thing in our lives—our relationship with Jesus Christ—we only have in common with Christians, and that automatically gives us a special relationship with another Christian. We can pray, read, and discuss God's Word together. We can talk about what the Lord is doing in our lives, and we can share prayer requests. These things we cannot do with an unsaved person.

Cultivating a casual relationship into a friendship takes a lot of time. To cultivate the friendship of Christians, you will need to get to know some of your children's friends at church (or at a Christian school, if they attend), and then invite the children over to spend time at your home or go on outings with your family. This may lead into doing things together with another Christian family, and even spending weekends together. This is a fantastic way to encourage Christian friendships that are deep, personal, and sustaining.

My husband is a nonbeliever, but is a good man in so many ways. How should I handle myself and my children in our daily relationships with him?

We hope that you will find the following suggestions to be helpful:

1. Submit to his wishes as long as you don't have to go against your beliefs. "Wives, submit yourselves unto your own husbands, as unto the Lord" (Eph. 5:22).

2. Show him what it means to be a Christian by your love for him and for your children. See John 13:34-35.

3. If he wants you to stay home from church on a particular Sunday to do something with him, do it!

4. Set a good example, but don't ever be patronizing in your attitude or actions toward him.

5. Please don't preach to him about his lack of faith, and don't act sanctimonious—both are guaranteed "turn-offs"!

6. Don't chastise him because he doesn't read the Bible or attend church, but when your church has some special event, invite him—casually—to go with you.

7. Don't insist upon his reading your latest and greatest inspirational books, but you may suggest a book every now and then that you feel would be meaningful to him.

8. Continue to tell your children what a wonderful father he is, and mean it!

9. Allow him to be the leader in your home in all but spiritual matters.

10. Encourage your children to pray for their father's salvation.

11. Pray for him yourself—constantly!

12. Ask the Lord to give you the proper attitude, guide your actions, and direct your words. This needs to be a daily prayer—sometimes even more often when things are rough! See Psalm 139:23-24.

13. Be comforted by the testimony of other women whose husbands have come to know the Lord because of "the behavior of the wives," as told us in 1 Peter 3:1.

Should children be spanked. With what? When?

We believe in "spanking" because it is biblical. For thousands of years, parents have been searching for a workable alternative to "spare the rod and spoil the child." From our observations, it has not yet been found. Such passages as Proverbs 23:13-14 and 29:15 confirm to parents that using the rod is both a proper and desirable method for changing behavior. Notice the use of the word "rod." This word occurs again and again, rather than the word "hand." We believe that the Lord intends us to use some type of instrument—not our hand. Our hands are to be associated with acts of love and service rather than fear and resentment.

However, the same Bible that admonishes us not to spare the rod also states just as strongly: "Fathers [parents], provoke not your children to anger, lest they be discouraged" (Col. 3:21). This is just as valid an admonition. Discipline must ALWAYS be done in love, with forethought and consistency. Bear in mind that lack of any discipline from parents also provokes children to anger.

One other thing—except in most extreme and unusual situations, discipline should be administered in private. For example, we find it very upsetting to watch mothers slapping a child in public when the child is misbehaving. Scolding loudly and slapping to the disgrace and embarrassment of both the child and mother is inexcusable. Standards need to be set before entering a public place. If a child forgets, a whispered but firm reminder should be given of what's in store at home unless the child behaves. If misbehavior continues, find a restroom—quickly!

I have two children, ages four and seven. When they receive birthday or Christmas presents, I insist that my older child write thank-you notes to express his gratitude, and that my four-year-old tell me what she wants to say, and I write her notes for her. I have been doing this since the children were two years old, and before that, I always made up notes and sent them. Their friends—Christian and non-Christian—do not write notes, but think it is sufficient to say a quick, "Thank you!" when the gift is given. My husband and I think that thank-you notes are important. Are we wrong?

We heartily agree with you. Galatians 5:22 tells us that one aspect of the fruit of the Spirit is kindness. Christians should be the most thoughtful and polite people in the world. Friends, neighbors, and relatives love to be thanked and shown appreciation. Your children are being trained properly, and you are doing the right thing. If your children should ever rebel about writing thank-you notes, simply tell them that your family does it because it is the kind and thoughtful thing for a Christian to do, and taking the time and effort to write a note shows extra appreciation for the gift received. After all, if a person had to take the time to shop for a gift, money to buy it, and more time and money to wrap it nicely and purchase an enclosure card, the very LEAST a child of God can do is to write a little thank-you note! Your family (and ours) may be among the last of the thank-you-note writers, but we will do it "heartily, as to the Lord" (Col. 3:23), showing our love and appreciation to others for what they have given to us.

Dinnertime preparations around our house are something to dread! Everyone is hungry and tired, and frankly, so am I. Any suggestions?

To help appease hunger pains get your children involved in the dinner preparations. The table needs to be set, and even a two-year-old can help with this by giving everyone a spoon or a napkin, or whatever. The older ones can fix the salad, stir something, open something else. Sure they are hungry, but the more they help, the faster preparations will be completed, and dinner can be served. Let some music cheer the house and you can all sing-a-long as you work—this may sound impossible, but it works. Bill Gaither's music is super before dinner, and any other time for that matter. Your spirits will revive, and you will be able to praise the Lord for your dinner and for your family.

My 11-year-old son has recently become lazy about doing various household jobs. He has cer-

*tain chores he's expected to do but he
doesn't finish or does a halfway job. Can you
help?*

Colossians 3:23-25 tells us that "Whatever you
do, do your work heartily, as for the Lord rather
than for men; knowing that from the Lord you
will receive the reward of the inheritance. It is
the Lord Christ whom you serve. For he who
does wrong will receive the consequences of the
wrong which he has done, and that without par-
tiality" (NASB).

Children need to learn the joy of a job well
done. Share these verses with your son and talk
to him about his responsibilities to your family
and to the Lord. Ask him what would happen if
your family did not do their various chores. What
if Dad only stayed at work until lunchtime,
though he was expected to work a full day? What
if Mom only cooked part of the dinner or cooked
it badly?

Most important of all, what if Jesus had not
done the work His Father expected of Him?
Where would all we sinners be?

6

Caution—Narrow Road Ahead

It's midnight. Do you know where YOUR child is? You should, but a more important question is: It's later than you think, do you know where YOUR child is going? Once your dimpled, cuddly baby grows up, your opportunities for guidance are limited. What will YOUR child do when you aren't around?

Proverbs 22:6 promises, "Train up a child in the way he should go; and when he is old, he will not depart from it." Our children will face many decisions now and in the future. They will also find that their beliefs are being constantly tested. Satan plays dirty! He doesn't follow rules! Our children can profit from making their own decisions and learning wisdom from their parents. They should be taught to weigh all the alternatives, to know all the facts, and to carefully determine the consequences of each alternative.

Parental training through the years must be aimed at preparing our children for this freedom.

When divine principles are interwoven in children, they will delight in doing God's will without parental prodding and nagging. We need to start at the earliest possible age to teach them self-discipline.

If we do as we're told in Ephesians 6:4 and bring our children up "in the discipline and instruction of the Lord" (NASB), our children will know which roads are open to them as they travel down the highway of life whether or not we're there to guide them!

Our child has a problem with self-confidence. Can you give us some ways to help him develop self-confidence?

Satan effectively hinders many Christians by destroying their self-confidence. We tend to become paralyzed and do nothing when the possibility of failure confronts us. In our children, this usually shows up as a hesitancy to assert themselves or to try new things.

In Isaiah 30:15, we read that God told the people of Israel that in "quietness and *confidence* shall your be your strength." The people of Israel became weak and ineffective when they lost confidence that the Lord was working through them, just as we do today. Proverbs 3:26 reminds us that "the Lord shall be thy *confidence.*" Philippians 1:6 adds that "Being *confident* of this very thing, that He which hath begun a good work in you will perform it until the day of Jesus Christ." It is evident from Scripture that the Lord intends us to have confidence—confidence not in ourselves alone, but in God as He works through us. Psalm 118:8 puts it this way, "It is better to trust in the Lord than to put confidence in man."

So, *self-confidence for a Christian is God-confidence.* Here are some specific suggestions for developing "God-confidence" in your child:

1. As Christians we are superloved and superblessed by the Lord Jesus Christ. Make sure that each of your children understands that he or she is "special" to you and to the Lord. Or as the Bill Gaither song puts it, "You are the only one of your kind." And then, because "special," he or she has been uniquely gifted by the Lord with capabilities to accomplish what no other individual can.

2. Respect each child for his uniqueness. He is not exactly like his parents, his brothers or sisters, or like anyone else who has ever lived—each child is different. Be a student of each of your children to discover his or her God-given capabilities or "bent" so that you can fashion your training to develop this "bent." Many times we parents attempt to mold our children to our own interests and/or abilities rather than to the individual child's. Classic examples are all about us: The frustrated mother who always wanted to be a musician forces her daughter to play a particular instrument; the rugged football player father who shoves his son into the football mold without waiting to discover if this is really "the way of the child."

3. Love each of your children with an unconditional love. This is a God-given kind of love. Does each of your children know that he is loved and accepted regardless of what he does? When each is disciplined he must understand that it is because you love him and want to teach him,

rather than that you are punishing him because "You embarrassed Mommy in front of her friends" or "You ruined Daddy's fishing gear."

4. Make your home the safest place in the world for your children. Each should be encouraged to experiment and be creative. The child should never be ridiculed when a project fails. Instead, he should always be helped and encouraged to improve and to try other things. It doesn't hurt once in a while to have a good laugh over a "goof" of your own, and then teach your children the lesson from your own failure. Give praise whenever you can genuinely give it, but don't oversell your children on their abilities. It can be a traumatic experience for a child, who has been led to believe that "he's the best" at something, to then suddenly discover in the real world that it just isn't so. If your children can trust your unconditional love and acceptance, you have created a psychologically safe climate in your home.

5. Spend time alone with each child, preferably every day, or—at least each week. This will be time when your attention is focused on what your child says, and on what he wants to do. This builds your child's self-esteem which leads to confidence because each learns that he is worth a special time—just for him. Susannah Wesley, mother of John Wesley, the famous Methodist theologian, had 12 children. She spent time alone with each of her 12 children—one hour each week! No, of course she didn't *have* the time—she made time! Her children were high on her priority list of "things to do."

6. Be patient. Building confidence is a long process. It takes years. As your child experiences

a measure of success in one area, it will give him confidence to try other things which may be increasingly more difficult.

What shall I tell my son when his friends jeer at and criticize our family's biblical beliefs? He's nine years old and quite articulate, but all his school friends are nonbelievers.

Often adults must face the same kind of persecution. God has promised us that "Blessed is a man who perseveres under trial; for once he has been approved, he will receive the crown of life, which the Lord has promised to those who love Him" (James 1:12, NASB). Christian children need to learn at a young age that being Christians often requires them to be "different" from other children. When a child chooses to receive Christ, he may also have to suffer for Christ's sake. The situation in which your son finds himself is a true test of his faith because at his particular age, he really needs his friends' approval. He will need strong faith, courage, self-discipline, and much, much prayer and encouragement during this trying time.

Remind your son of the story of Noah who built the ark under difficult circumstances, as recorded in Genesis 6. Noah and his family were the only ones who were saved from the flood because they believed what God told them. It's difficult to be the only one or even to be part of a minority. It takes great faith and courage to stand up to a jeering crowd. "Every careless word that men shall speak, they shall render account for it in the day of judgment" (Matt. 12:36, NASB). Your son might be reassured by the example of Peter and the

Apostles who faced a similar situation in Acts 5:29 when they decided, "We must obey God rather than men" (NASB).

Paul also suffered greatly at the hands of unbelievers. He reminds us to "Be on the alert, stand firm in the faith, act like men, be strong. Let all that you do be done in love" (1 Cor. 16:13-14, NASB).

As you help your son pray about this test of his faith, ask the Lord to give him wisdom and help him feel love for his unsaved friends and to remember to "Consider it all joy when you encounter various trials, knowing that the testing of your faith produces endurance" (James 1:2-3, NASB).

My children are now ages nine and six and the Lord has recently revealed to me how harmful TV is. How can I effectively begin to wean my children away from it—especially my son who has been more or less raised on TV?

This will be a long, slow process, but it's well worth the effort. So be patient, but firm. Ask God to change your children's attitudes and dependence upon the tube, and to give you wisdom in speaking to them. After paving the way with prayer, you will want to tell the children how you feel, and why this change has taken place in your attitude.

Don't expect them to jump for joy or even understand the change. Remember, the TV is probably their main interest in life—or close to it. This, of course, is one reason it is so harmful and has such an effect upon children's thinking and actions.

Prayerfully decide together which programs may be watched—preferably not more than one per evening. You will need to plan alternate activities for the time that they formerly spent watching TV. And—be prepared—you will need to spend a large portion of this time with them. Ask the children what they would like to do, but plan ahead and have some of your own suggestions ready. Reading books aloud as a family, doing puzzles together, playing "hide-n-seek," bikeriding, building things together, playing various indoor and outdoor games are some possible suggestions. Be *sure* to let your children know that you plan to spend this extra time doing things with them. This will make the "break" less painful!

Why is it that some children who have been raised in Christian homes seem to "go wrong" in their teen years? What happens? How can we prevent this?

We worked with a core group of about 20 children in a Bible-teaching church over a period of ten years. We observed them when they were 3 and 4, again when they were 9, 10, and 11, and again when they were 13. Some of them seemed to become "immunized" to Christianity. In all cases one or more of these six factors were present.

1. Some had never accepted the Lord as their personal Saviour, but knew all the common Christian cliches. This is one reason why it is so vital that our children sincerely come to know and love the Lord at an early age before they "just learn the language."

2. Some came from very legalistic, rule-bound homes, where they had to walk through the Christian life on eggshells, without enjoying it at all. And what did the kids learn? They learned that the Christian life is not fun, so, "I don't want it, and when I'm old enough, I'm going," and—they went. We've talked with them, and they are bitter and resentful.

3. Some came from homes at the opposite extreme where there was very little discipline. Either the parents didn't care, were too busy, or had been duped into believing the lie that you should let children "do their own thing"—i.e. "You don't want to thwart them because it will damage their psyche." Kids that come from these homes are just as bitter and resentful as those who came from the superlegalistic homes. Proverbs 3:12 tells us that when parents love their children they will correct them, just as the Lord corrects those He loves and in whom He takes delight.

4. Some of them came from hypocritical homes, which the kids detected quickly. Such a home can be illustrated like this: A family is having devotions, and the father has asked, "Steve, what does the Bible say about lying?" Steve answers, "The Bible says that a lie is an abomination unto the Lord, and. . . ." Just then the telephone rings. The father answers it. Billy listens as his dad doesn't really tell a lie but s-t-r-e-t-c-h-e-s the truth to the nth degree. He then comes back and asks again, "Now what is it that the Bible says about lying, Steve?" Steve smiles and answers, "A lie is an abomination unto the Lord, and—a very present help in time of trouble, huh, Dad?" The Christian life held no

reality for this father. Can you blame the son for not wanting it?

We do have a pattern for establishing a home with a real, vital, and practical relationship with the Lord. It is found in Deuteronomy 6:5-7: "And thou shalt love the Lord thy God with all thine heart, and with all thy soul, and with all thy might. And these words, which I command thee this day, shall be in thine heart; and thou shalt teach them diligently unto thy children, and shalt talk of them when thou sittest in thine house, and when thou walkest by the way, and when thou liest down, and when thou risest up." The parents' example of genuine commitment to the Word of God is crucial. Parents so committed will provide a consistent and constant flow of God-loving training in the home.

An example of this kind of home is related by Corrie ten Boom in her book, *In My Father's House* (Revell, © 1976).

> When I was five years old, I learned to read. I loved stories, particularly those about Jesus. He was a member of the ten Boom family. It was just as easy to talk to Him as it was to carry on a conversation with my mother and father, my aunts, or my brother and sisters. He was there.

5. Some of them never learned to use leisure time wisely. How are you teaching your children to use leisure time in your home? How do you use it? You are setting the pattern for them. Is their leisure time filled with the violence and evil imaginations found in many TV programs, movies, or books that have not been chosen carefully? Or do you guide them carefully in their use

of leisure time? Are your children busy with household chores, family projects and games, and recreational activities done together?

Plan for summer vacation like a military man might plan a complicated maneuver, but with the children having their input. When your child says, "There's nothing to do!" and he seems to have done all that you suggest, have a special and different project for him to work on. For example, he might begin to work on Christmas presents for the family. Certainly he has more time in the summer than during the busy fall months. Maybe he can be learning a new sport, such as playing tennis, which takes unlimited practice. Trips to the library, the park, and outings with friends as well as bicycle excursions with the family are examples of ways some have found helpful in taking care of leisure time. Learning to play an instrument, potting, labeling, and taking care of plants, cultivating a vegetable garden, reading books on gardening, training and building a home for a new puppy, making an illustrated diary of summer outings and trips, and memorizing portions of God's Word are only a few suggestions. You and your children will find many more.

6. Some of them chose the wrong friends. Earnestly pray that the Lord will give your children one or more special Christian friends. He has answered that prayer in many families we know of, and He will for you. Encourage your children to participate in church-sponsored events, and to invite their friends from the church to your home.

What about Santa Claus? How can a Christian family handle "him"?

Santa Claus is here to stay as long as there are things to sell, stores to sell them, and people to buy. Everywhere you go in December he's there—padded, red, and, on occasion, jolly. It doesn't seem reasonable to ignore him—you can't and your young children won't.

The attitude many parents convey to their children (and it works) is that in December, Santa Claus appears, and there are a lot of fairy tales (stories that are make-believe, not true) about him and his reindeer. He's in the stores, and if the children want to tell him what they would like to have for Christmas, that's OK, but it's just for fun. If they don't care to talk to him so much the better. The family won't have to stand in line.

These families do not advocate giving presents from "Santa," leaving cookies and milk, or having a lot of Santa regalia around the house. All these things detract from the Lord Jesus Christ and will lessen the Christmas impact you want in your home at this time of year. Being honest with your children will not "ruin" Christmas for them, but will make them feel grown-up and way ahead of their duped peers!

I need ideas on how to give each child individual building up so he'll learn self-confidence. Mine are seven, five, and three.

Here are some ideas that have worked successfully in many families:

1. Treat your children as INDIVIDUALS. That means absolutely no comparing of achievements and aspirations. God has made each one different, and has a tailor-made plan for each life. Let each of your children know that you really

enjoy being with him or her. You must mean this, so if you have a problem with favoritism, take it to the Lord. He can change your attitudes and give you the spirit of love and joy you need to communicate to your children. Have fun with each child. Treat each as a real person, and ask for his opinion or advice concerning such things as menu ideas, vacation plans, recreational activities, decorating, gardening, etc. Let each child be a part of planning your home life. This gives status in a hurry. If a child's idea is impossible for whatever reason, explain why to the child, and suggest modifications of the idea which will make it workable.

2. Compliment your children for the positive things they do (ask the Lord to reveal these to you). Do it individually and in front of the entire family. When you compliment one child in front of the entire family, make CERTAIN that you have a compliment for each child, or at least even up the compliments over a very short period of time. Otherwise resentments and hostilities will arise.

3. In your family prayertime thank God for each child individually and for what each one contributed to the family or to friends that day. For example, you might thank God that Jerry helped Susie put her shoes on the right feet, and that Susie is learning to dry the dishes. For example, thank God that Billy is doing better in handwriting at school, or that the teacher told you that Steve was a good helper today.

4. Assign to each of your children tasks within the child's ability to perform. This will make each of them feel that he is an important member óf the team, both wanted and needed. Inciden-

tally, this will also show the importance of seem-ingly simple assignments, such as setting the ta-ble. How can one eat without a knife, fork, and spoon?

5. Lavish praise on each child when it is de-served. Prayerfully discuss negative things, but, please, only one negative at a time. Doesn't the Lord work that way with us, knowing that most of us can work on only one area of our lives at a time?

6. Encourage each child to get involved in a variety of activities. Point out that the Lord has made each with the capacity and capability to enjoy many different things. Each needs to learn that participation in areas where he may not excel can sometimes be just as much fun and worth-while as those in which he does excel.

What about tantrums?

Almost every child goes through some type of tantrum stage. The length of that stage depends a lot on the parents' reactions. If at all possible, completely ignore the tantrum. Ask the Lord to give you the patience to do this. Tantrum-givers revel in having an audience. Try your best to act as if nothing is happening! Leave the immediate area if possible. Tantrum-givers do not like to stage a performance with no one around—after all, tantrums are a lot of work!

If the circumstances are such that you cannot ignore the tantrum, then you must let your child know that you will not tolerate this behavior, and you may need to administer the "rod." Your child must be made to realize that having a tantrum is not the technique to use to get his way in this

world. Regardless of the supposed embarrassment to you, do NOT give in to him. Haven't you
seen adults who lose their tempers over nothing,
throw things, shout obscenities, and generally act
like overgrown two-year-olds? You can be certain
that this behavior was either learned and reinforced in their homes at an early age or not dealt
with at all.

7

Three Little Words

Preteens and teenagers can be distressingly and disarmingly honest in their evaluations of us parents! And what often hurts the most is that they are all too frequently "right on target"!

During the past couple of years we have asked well over 100 junior highers, mostly from Christian homes, to answer these four questions in approximately 200 words:

1. What is a family?
2. What are the good things about a family?
3. What are the bad things about a family?
4. What will you do when you are a parent?

The young people were encouraged to be honest, and told that it was not necessary to put their names on their papers. There was absolutely NO discussion of possible answers that might have swayed their responses!

Their answers, written by approximately 50 girls and 60 boys, have been a revelation. In almost every paper three words were mentioned, and in some cases these three words were repeated again and again and again.

The words were *love, talk,* and *together.* Over and over again the young people expressed a desire to be loved and appreciated, to have a home where parents would listen to ideas and be willing to discuss them without fighting, downgrading, or sarcasm. They longed for a home where parents would spend time with them, doing things that the young person chose to do, and to have parents who really enjoyed being with them.

The only way to give you the true picture of the desire of these junior highers' hearts is just to share with you some direct quotes from their papers to the questions we asked.

1. *What is a family?*
"To me a family is not just a group of people living under one roof. A family is, of course, a father and mother and the younger and older children. But that's not all. A family shows many things such as love, respect, and responsibility. And the family helps one another. Like if you had some homework and you didn't understand a question you could always go and talk to an older brother or sister if you had one. A family is supposed to have relationships together and to go places together, not just, 'I want to go here.' A lot of time the word 'I' is a word that messes up a family for good!"

"A family should be able to talk with each other and discuss problems or decisions. A family should also be close together to talk about the Word of God. They should listen to each other discuss matters instead of saying that something is dumb and the way you tell it is all wrong."

"A family is a group of people that try to stick together and help each other. They should love one another and try to teach each other what they know. The Bible sets down rules and regulations for the members of the family, and I think each member of the family should try to follow these to make their families happier."

"A family is a group of people brought together by love. There is a very special feeling in their hearts to depend on each other for warmth and love. A family is something special."

"A family is people. Kids, mother and father. Families do things together and go places together. Some families are separated and some aren't. A family should be together. A family should also love God. Families should protect one another and care for one another. If a family loves God they will be a better family."

2. *What are the good things about a family?*
"The good things about a family are the way they help each other with their problems. They share their life with each other. The family cares to help each other with the small problems and the big problems in life. They all respond when you talk to them."

"They can do things. If someone in the family has a problem someone can help him. They can share everything. If you have something on your mind you have a family to talk about it with, to pray with about it. A family can laugh together, and cry together."

"I'm glad that I am in a Christian family. In other families I see kids running around backtalking to their parents and other things. I'm just glad that I'm controlled and loved instead of being left alone to live by myself."

"The good thing about a family is the way of being together, and having fun together. Usually when one person in the family is having fun, the other people in the family enjoy it too. When there is love throughout the family, the whole family has fun together. It is almost like an empathy."

3. *What are the bad things about a family?*
"I don't think parents should be a bad example to young children, or children of any age. Children want to be just like their parents, and what good is smoking and drinking going to do them? Children need love and support from their parents and if they can't get it from them, they will try to get it elsewhere. Growing up in an atmosphere of hate is bad for a child, and so is a life of stealing, cheating, and lying. I think that if these are in the home then the family is to blame, and that family is no good. Lazy, unloving, uncaring parents and parents that are gone a lot are not good. Remember—your home is what you make it, so try to keep it the way God would want it."

"The bad things in a family are hate, anger, and fighting. They are not close at all. They don't talk to each other, or they don't do anything together, and they aren't very friendly at all.

"The bad things about a family are when they separate their lives from each other and don't really care about the other ones' feelings. They don't help or really respond to each other's feelings. They don't tell each other their faults so they can help each other improve."

"The bad things of a family are when the family is never together, and always doing their own thing because when you always do your own thing you are never with your family so you don't grow together, and if you are doing your own thing when you are not around your parents and there is no discipline and a good family needs discipline."

"The bad thing about a family is when the parents are ignoring the children or not really trying to listen to what they are trying to say!"

"The bad things are when the parents have bad disputes, raise their children wrong, beat them without purpose, not caring, not loving, not providing, and worst of all—not Christians."

4. *What will you do when you are a parent?* "When I am a parent I will spend lots of time with my kids. I won't spoil them, but I will give them many things. When there is a problem in my family, I will talk it out. I will go to church with my kids and I will try to make them good Christians."

"I wouldn't yell at my children. I would have talks with them and explain why it isn't right to do bad things. If they didn't learn by these talks I would discipline them. I would tell them that I love them. If they have problems at school or with friends, I would ask them if they want to talk about it. If they don't want to talk about the problems, I would tell them I care about them and their problems, just as Jesus cares about His children. Then I would sit and talk with them and try to help them with their problems."

"When I am a parent I will always look back at my past and think what my parents did for discipline and other things, and think if it did any good or not. If it did good, then I will use the same, and if it didn't then I will give him or her a punishment that suits the crime."

"I think when I'm a parent I will discipline my children enough so they won't be spoiled, but not a lot so they will hate me. We'll go together to parks and to ice cream parlors, and things like that. I'll live in a cozy house, and once in a while, especially when it's raining, have a fire, and pop popcorn. I think when I'm a parent, I'm going to have fun with my children!"

Well, that's what these junior highers want, and to a great extent, that's what we want too. These young people had a way of filtering through all the extraneous "stuff" that comprises family living, and of getting down to the basics.

Our concluding questions deal with these basics, as have the vast majority of questions in this book. Our prayer is that the Lord will lead and guide you in making your dwelling place a home where God is loved, His Word is honored, and where His love and His Word permeate your thoughts, actions, and words.

Our second child was just born. We have been so distressed by seeing brothers and sisters in our friends' families fighting and quarreling constantly. Is there any way to keep from having such problems?

Very realistically you must realize that "when there are siblings, there are going to be quibblings." It's a fact of life since neither parents nor children are perfect, and everyone is sinful.

Here are four principles to follow which help to lessen sibling rivalry:

1. Use consistent discipline with your children. Parents often protect the younger child and punish the older regardless of which is at fault. This is unfair and unjust to both children, and they will react accordingly. Rather, let the children know that to the best of your ability you are trying to be fair and impartial. When you discover you've made an error, apologize to the children, and be sincere! Also, in your family prayertime, acknowledge to the Lord when you are in error, and ask His forgiveness and His help in doing the right thing with your children. In that way your children will realize how genuinely sorry you are, that you wish to have the Lord's forgiveness as well as theirs, and that you need His help and guidance in doing your job as a parent, just as they need Him in their lives. This will be an example of confession, according to 1 John 1:9, that they can use too.

2. Give each child individual attention and time everyday—time to listen to needs and problems, time to share a joke or a joy, or time to play a game. This is difficult, but not impossible, and you must do it! Each child will recognize what

you are doing (if not, tell him—a two-year-old will understand!), and each will learn to respect his brother or sister's time with you.

3. Do NOT compare achievements and aspirations—please! Want to have a lot of problems? Comparing and belittling is the fastest way to cause unhappiness and friction between children (adults too!). Regardless of the number of children you may have, each will be different and unique. Comparing them becomes an exercise in futility. Just enjoy each child—each will be better because of it!

4. Every day in your family prayertime, thank God for each child and for something he has done that day. This welds a family together, and gives respect for each individual as a person and for the accomplishments of each. We make it a rule to also ask the Lord to give us more love for Him, His Word, and each other. We believe He answers.

We want to keep the lines of communication open with our children now, through adolescence, and beyond. Can you give us any practical suggestions for doing this?

First, last, and always—listen, LISTEN, L-I-S-T-E-N! You can do plenty of communicating without ever saying a word. Does your manner indicate that you really want to hear what happened, or is your mind on your own affairs? Do you listen carefully and enthusiastically? Are you a critical listener or an accepting and understanding one? Most importantly, if a child is in trouble of some kind, or has done something wrong, don't "jump" all over him. This will forever close the lines of communication just when they are most needed. Instead, guide and help the child through the problem.

You must be interested in what interests your children at whatever age they are. When your two-year-old gets thrilled with a flower, you too should be delighted, and look for more flowers to make arrangements and centerpieces for family dinners. When your seven-year-old is "into" T-ball, you (either or both parents) should go to the games, notice his improvement, practice with him at home and/or in the park, and have family T-ball games, if possible. When your children earn their 10-speed-bicycles, you should investigate the bikeways available in your city and nearby towns, and plan weekend jaunts and picnics with other bike-riding friends. Basketball season should find you in the stands or on the sidelines, showing interest and support. Whatever your child's area of interest, make it apparent that you want to learn with your child, even though it may not be your "thing." In doing this you will also find that your children, in turn, will become interested in your activities and accept them.

Your children may be reluctant to "tell all" when you ask the inevitable, "What did you do in school today?" "Nothing much," may be their answer. Don't be discouraged. Your children may need some recovery time before they are ready to verbalize and share with you. A snack after school usually opens up communication lines a bit earlier.

Your morning breakfast and prayertime together is a great way to bridge the gap between morning and evening happenings. Take about five minutes to talk about and pray for the things that are important in each person's life that day. For example, Rion's math test, Gary's T-Ball game, Candi's part in the school play, Daddy's job interview, Mommy's home Bible study are the important things to the members of a family on a particular day, and need to be taken to the Lord in prayer. Then in the evening, a time of sharing is normal, natural, and expected because everyone has prayed together earlier in the day. Now you can share and thank God for what He has done that day.

My five-year-old son is always asking questions. I know I'm an impatient person and that I don't take the time to talk to him as much as I should, but he really gets on my nerves. I love my son, but I have difficulty showing him that I do at times. Any suggestions?

Ask the Lord to make you more patient in dealing with your son and to enable you to show him the love you feel for him. We all feel frustrated and impatient at times. Children seem to know when we're the busiest or pressured and that's when they tend to demand more of our time.

It is often a problem of priorities. We need to remember that it's sometimes better to leave those dishes in the sink or that bed unmade rather than to leave an unanswered concern or question in our child's heart. We are always asking God for things yet He sets the supreme example of patience for us. Our Lord showed great patience in dealing with those who had difficulty believing He was the Messiah. He had to tell people the same things over and over just as we tell our children the same things over and over.

If our children find us too busy to talk with them, we may be losing the opportunity to cement that bond of communication which is so crucial during the adolescent years. They may also feel that if we're too busy to deal with them, God may be too. Again . . . the parental example.

Some children really are more irritating and harder to love than others, but we need to pray about this and the Lord will abundantly answer. God still loves us when we are "naughty" . . . and our children need the same reassurance of our unconditional love for them.

There is so much to do and so little time. How can my wife and I make the best use of the time we have on a daily basis?

The following *JUST FOR TODAY* checklist has been helpful to many parents:
- ☐ Did I thank God for each of my children?
- ☐ Did I laugh and enjoy my children?
- ☐ Did I spend time alone with each child?
- ☐ Did I praise each of my children for something special?
- ☐ Did our family do something together as a family unit?
- ☐ Did our family share at least one mealtime together?
- ☐ Did I discuss and/or read a book with each child?
- ☐ Did I take time to listen—really listen—when my children wanted to talk?
- ☐ Did I pray with my children and for my children?

☐ Did I relate the time we spent in the Word to each child's need and spiritual level?

☐ Did I demonstrate love for each of my children?

☐ Did each child's response indicate that he is confident of my love?

☐ Did I share with my spouse what I learned about each child?

☐ Did I have a good idea of what my children were doing and with whom they were at any hour of the day?

☐ Did I use the special time I had with my children in the best way to accomplish growth toward the ultimate goals for them?

And finally in summary ...
Ten Tips for Parents

1. Remember that God does **NOT** waste parents on children—or children on parents. He gave you each special child because of what you can bring to the life of that child, and because of what He will use each child to teach and develop in you.

2. Never let your children cause you to neglect your spouse—that is not in God's plan. Remember that you will be a parent in the operational sense for about 18 to 25 years but, God willing, you will be a spouse from 40 to 60 years. A most basic security for children comes from knowing that their parents love and respect each other.

3. Researchers tell us that 50% of a child's attitudes and habits are established by the time the child is four years old, and 80% by the time he is eight. Do not ever underestimate the importance

of what you are teaching your children every day—including their first months of life—long before they can say, "Daddy, Mommy, I love you!"

4. God created each of your children as a unique individual—the world has never had one quite like any of them before, and never will again. So—if each has been created by God to be different from everyone else, it is just possible that each of your children will not sit up, crawl, get a first tooth, or walk at precisely the same time as you did, or as your best friend's child, or as the children of the couple across the street. Why should you care? God knows what He's doing with you and with your children, and His timing is best!

5. Get your priorities regarding your time and energy settled right now—it will save you grief, regrets, and wasted later years. Which is going to get the most time: Your friends or your children? Your churchwork or your children? Your outside interests or your children? Your housework or your children? A balance is needed, and is often difficult to achieve. Ask the Lord to give you wisdom and understanding in establishing and maintaining the schedule that is right for YOU! (not for your friends, or the neighbors, or the boys and girls at church, but for YOU).

6. Consistent discipline isn't easy, and when you are tired, busy, and preoccupied with life's various emergencies and demands, it becomes increasingly difficult. But it is essential—if you become too busy or too tired to discipline properly, then it's time to start eliminating some of those other "things" from your life—fast! A child of six to nine months understands "No!" and can

learn to obey. A child of 6- or 9- or 16-years will never understand why something is "No!" sometimes and "OK" at other times. Be firm, be consistent. Mean what you say—each and every time!

7. Rearing our children "In the nurture and admonition of the Lord" is an awesome responsibility. But, the Lord never intended for us to muddle through alone—He's there to lead and to guide. He will give the wisdom you need when you need it, if you will but ask. Raising a Christian is a "prayer affair" each day—many times.

8. If you really love your children so that each child knows and understands what love is and how it operates in your home as you "show and tell" it, nothing of material value you withhold from your children will matter. Likewise, there is nothing of material value that you can give your children to compensate for a lack of love. Correctional institutions are filled with young men and women who never felt really "loved" or that they "mattered" or that anyone cared what they did as long as they stayed out of the way.

9. The expression, "Do as I say, not as I do," has no place in the Christian home. "What you do speaks so loudly that I cannot hear what you say" is the natural behavioral response that children will make. What we say on the telephone when we assume no one is listening, how we talk to our spouse, to our friends, to people in stores, and even the tone of voice we use and the very attitudes we have are the examples our children will emulate.

We parents need to strive to be, with God's help, the model of what we want our children to be. In the vast majority of cases, children do NOT rise above the parental examples.

10. Please—parents—let's enjoy our children! Have fun with them from the day they are born. And then in every following day learn to laugh with them, play with them, and listen to them. By the way, parenthood is less of a burden and more of a joy if we keep our sense of humor. Spilled milk is less of a chore, spitting up is less of a nuisance, the inevitable childhood illnesses are more bearable if we keep our sense of humor, and just enjoy each child during every passing—never to return—stage of development.